Instant Idea Book

Holidays and Seasons
Easy-to-Use Activities
for Elementary Teachers

by
Barbara Gruber

illustrations
Ed Salmon

Copyright© 1985 Frank Schaffer Publications, Inc.
All rights reserved - Printed in the U.S.A.
Published by **Frank Schaffer Publications, Inc.**
1028 Via Mirabel, Palos Verdes Estates, California 90274

ISBN #0-86734-055-X

Table of Contents

Introduction

Holidays and Seasons—Easy-to-Use Activities is filled with quick, creative ideas. They are all classroom-tested and will be of high interest to your students.

Pages 6-12 contain simple directions for projects mentioned throughout the book. I have also included many learning activities you can use all year long in your classroom.

Keep this book on your desk! It will be a source of many wonderful learning experiences in your classroom.

Barbara Gruber

Barbara Gruber

Directions for projects in this book

Clay Dough

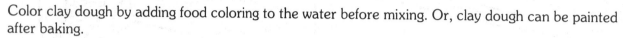

Mix 1 cup flour and 1/2 cup salt.
Add 1/3 cup water, a little at a time.
Squeeze dough with your hands until smooth.
Store in plastic bag until ready to use.

If too crumbly, add small amount of water.
If too wet, add small amount of flour.

Color clay dough by adding food coloring to the water before mixing. Or, clay dough can be painted after baking.

Clay dough objects can be air-dried or baked at 225° for approximately thirty minutes. Thick objects will need to be baked longer.

Paper Quilts

Cut a piece of butcher paper approximately 3′ x 6′ for quilt backing. Give each student a 10″ square of white paper for his quilt square. Paste finished paper squares on the quilt backing, leaving the backing show between squares.

Paper Quilt Ideas:

animals
holiday symbols
patriotic symbols
flags
birds
flowers
inventions
presidents
famous women
famous black people/history
signs of fall
signs of winter
signs of spring

Inexpensive Instant Photographs

Use a photocopier to make extra copies of your class photograph or students' pictures. You will get a black and white copy from color photographs.

Sand Tables or Dioramas

Use kitty litter for the "ground" material in sand tables or dioramas. It comes in an earth tone or green.

FS-8305   Instant Idea Book

Directions for projects in this book

Learning Bookmarks

Cut tagboard or construction paper in strips 2" or 3" x 12".
Students have space to illustrate and write on this size bookmark.

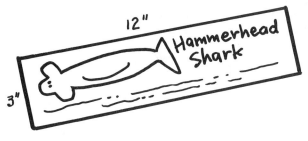 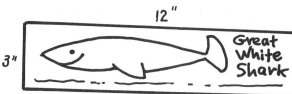

Booklets

Use wallpaper samples for the covers of writing booklets.
Make booklets in different sizes and shapes.

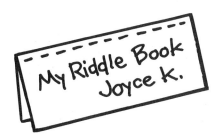  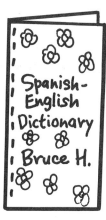 

Accordian Books

Cut a strip of paper 4" x 18".
Fold in half two times, then fanfold on creases.
Paste a tagboard cover on each end of the accordian book.
Use books for writing stories, poems, riddles . . .

Word Hunts and Crossword Puzzles

Use graph paper for making word hunts or crossword puzzles.
You and your students will find this to be a helpful hint.

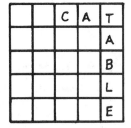 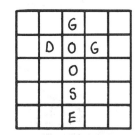 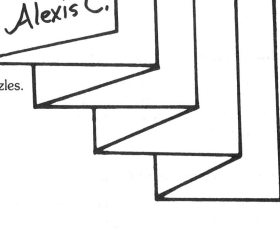

 FS-8305   Instant Idea Book

Directions for projects in this book

Mobiles—the easy way!

Use a wire clothes hanger for student mobiles.
A stripped umbrella makes a good frame for a large mobile.

Super-size Postage Stamps

Draw a postage stamp on a duplicating master.
Students cut on dotted lines to make perforations.
To make stamps sturdier, students can do their
illustrations on construction paper rectangles and
paste them in the center on the stamp.

Quickie Paper Puppets

Fold 12″ x 18″ construction paper into thirds, lengthwise.
Then fold into fourths.
Fold in half so open ends are on the outside for inserting fingers.
Paste on features using paper, yarn or other materials.

Handy Hang-Ups

Looking for another spot to hang charts, posters and mobiles?
Put magnetic cup hooks under chalk ledge and use the empty wall space under the chalkboards.

©Frank Schaffer Publications, Inc.

Directions for projects in this book

Parent Notes

Create instant forms for parent communication.
Tuck these handy notes inside your desk for quick use.

Stack-a-Box File

Label empty ditto master boxes with the names of the months.
Stack the boxes and use to store masters for seasonal and holiday worksheets.

Snip-and-Save Baskets

It's easy for students to lose pieces of art projects when they are cutting and pasting.
Keep a stack of plastic berry baskets handy. Each student can put one on his desk when doing an art project. Students can use the baskets for all the pieces they don't want to lose or accidentally throw away.

9

Learning Activities for any holiday or season

A Decorated Plant

Keep a plant in your classroom in a bright spot.
Decorate the plant with paper "ornaments"
according to the season or holiday. Decorations
can be hung from branches of the plant or
taped to a stick or wire. Or, you can stand a
twig or branch in a flowerpot with plaster of
paris. Ornaments can be hung from the branch.

Ideas for paper ornaments:

leaves
pumpkins, witches and ghosts
flowers
shamrocks
snowflakes
birds
hearts

Fancy Bulletin Boards

Large paper tablecloths decorated with holiday
or seasonal motifs are perfect for covering
bulletin boards. Look for half-price bargains on
these in stationery and variety stores on the day
after a holiday.

"What's Next" Calendar Symbols

Cut out calendar symbols in different colors (September: leaves in
red, gold, yellow and light brown).
Establish a sequence as you add a symbol to the calendar each day.
Ask students which color comes next.

Poetry Page

Copy a poem about a season or holiday on a large piece
of paper.
Have a student decorate a border or add an illustration to
the poetry page.
Post the poem and read it aloud together frequently.
You'll be delighted at how quickly your students memo-
rize the poem.
You might want to have a different poem for the class to
learn each month.
Post poetry pages around the classroom for students to
reread.
Perhaps the wall space below the chalk ledge can be used.
Save poetry pages to reuse.

Learning Activities for any occasion

Please Touch Display

Have a table or area in the classroom where books and items can be displayed.
Encourage students to bring objects for the "Please Touch" display.

Little People

Make tagboard patterns for students to trace people and clothing. Have each child cut a paper person from tagboard.
Students make the paper person look like themselves by drawing facial features and pasting on yarn or colored paper for hair.
Students dress the paper cutouts according to the season or holiday. Attach pattern pieces with a dab of paste.
Paper cutouts are posted on a bulletin board or wall and are used all year long.

Ideas for dressing paper cutouts:

Halloween costume for fall
Pilgrim boy or girl
famous person
what student wants to be when grown up
coat and hat for winter
leprechaun
raincoat for spring
shorts and T-shirt for summer

Special Shape Books

Shape books make writing activities special for students at any grade level.
Make shape books with construction paper covers and lined paper inside.

September:	leaf, apple, school bus
October:	pumpkin, ghost, haunted house
November:	cornucopia, turkey, Pilgrim boy or girl
December:	candy cane, tree, gift box, Santa, menorah
January:	tree, snowman, mitten
February:	heart, silhouette of Lincoln/Washington
March:	shamrock, kite, lion, lamb
April:	egg, bunny, chick, rabbit, basket, umbrella
May:	flower, fish, bird, frog, baseball
June:	sun, picnic basket, clown, flag, butterfly

FS-8305 Instant Idea Book

Add your ideas to each list!

Things to make

model
mural
series of pictures
time line
poster
mobile
map
greeting card
gift wrap
postage stamp
costume
diorama
coupon book
puppet
collage
comic strip
mask
game
food

Writing Activities

story
poem
play
riddles, jokes
questions and answers
report
paragraph
directions
diary
letter
secret code
invitation
word dictionary
picture dictionary

Oral Language Activities

read orally
recite a poem
give a play
make a tape
conduct an interview
participate in choral speaking
sing a song
give an oral report

FS-8305   Instant Idea Book

Learning Activities for September, October and November

©Frank Schaffer Publications, Inc.

FS-8305   Instant Idea Book

Fall Activities

Summer Is Over, Fall Is Here!

Buy a pumpkin and bring it to school. Cut an opening in the top that is large enough to hold a jar. Scoop out the pulp and insert a jar filled with water. Put branches of colorful fall leaves in the pumpkin.

Beautiful Leaves

Encourage students to bring colorful fall leaves to school. Leaves can be pressed and mounted in a scrapbook. Leaves should be placed inside tissue, or paper towels, and between the pages of a book. Place something heavy on the book, so leaves are pressed flat. A collage of pressed leaves can be arranged on a bulletin board or piece of art paper.

The Weather Is Changing

Record on the classroom calendar the time of sunrise and sunset, and the high and low temperatures for each day. This information is published daily in the newspaper. Let students take turns writing the data on the calendar. Discuss the changing weather patterns.

Leaf Rubbings

Make leaf rubbings by placing a paper over a leaf and rubbing lightly with a crayon. A "skeleton" of the leaf will appear. Leaf rubbings can be cut out and used for art projects and bulletin boards.

FS-8305   Instant Idea Book

Fall Activities

Poetry About the Fall Season

Jot poetry starters on the chalkboard or on construction paper leaf shapes. Students can select one and finish writing the poem:

Nights are cool,
Days are short . . .

Some leaves are red,
Some leaves are gold . . .

Fall is here,
Leaves are coming down . . .

Squirrels are busy now,
Hiding nuts, everywhere . . .

Summer is over,
Fall is here . . .

Rake the leaves,
Make a big pile . . .

It was cold last night,
Winter is on its way . . .

Fall Colors by the Yard

Following directions, measuring skills and creativity are all included in this interesting activity with a fall theme. Give each student a 3" x 36" strip of white paper. (You can cut butcher paper into strips or use a roll of adding machine paper.) Write directions on the chalkboard for decorating the paper strip with crayons or felt markers. (Begin measurement at "0".)

Measure 2 inches:	Write your name in your favorite color.
5 ½ inches:	Draw a colorful fall leaf.
8 inches:	Make a brown, gold and orange design using circles.
4 inches:	Write FALL IS HERE! in fall colors.
5 inches:	Make a red, yellow and gold design using triangles.
6 ½ inches:	Draw a pumpkin patch.
5 inches:	Make a design using circles, squares and triangles in three different colors.

(Increase the difficulty of this activity by making measurement segments and pictures more difficult.)

FS-8305   Instant Idea Book

Welcome Back to School!

Get the school year off to the best start ever.

Handprints and Footprints

Each student traces his handprint or footprint on construction paper. Be sure to have students write their names on the papers. Assign students to a partner, so they can help each other with tracing.

Collect papers and cut out prints. Add an extra piece or two of construction paper in different colors, so you are actually cutting out several of each child's handprint at one time. Do the same for the footprints. Use a felt pen to print each child's name on his handprints and footprints.

Use handprints for borders around bulletin boards.

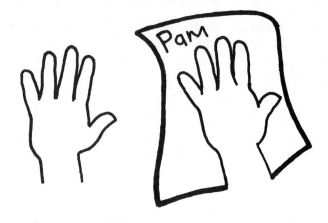

(See Hand-In-Hand Idea on page 21.)

Guess Who?

Each student writes about herself without revealing her name. Directions to students: Tell if you are a boy or girl, what you look like, what your hobbies are and what kind of person you are. Have students write their names on the backs of their papers and papers are collected. Read aloud a paper and classmates try to guess whose paper is being read.

All About Me!

Have students write a letter to you telling you about themselves.

My name is _____,
I am _____ years old.
My hobby is _____
_____ . At school. I
do my best work in _____
_____.
I need some help in _____
_____.
My favorite thing at school
is _____.
                    Sincerely,
                _____

Working Together Is Fun!

A group activity is a wonderful way for students to get to know each other. Divide students into groups of five or six students. Give each group a large piece of paper (approximately 3' x 4') to make a montage. Assign each group a different topic for its montage. Students cut pictures of their subject from old magazines and take turns pasting them onto the montage. Pictures can be any size and may be overlapped. Montage subjects can be faces, people, animals, cars, foods . . .

FS-8305   Instant Idea Book

Native American Day

The fourth Friday of September is a special day to honor American Indians.

Native American tribes used materials found in nature for clothing, food and shelter. Therefore, the Indian way of life varied from region to region and tribe to tribe. Help your students learn the many different ways Native Americans lived long ago and the way they live today.

Post a map of the United States. Use felt markers to indicate Indian regions.

How They Lived

Learn about the ways Native Americans lived. Divide your class into study groups or work together as a class.

*Have each group study Indian life in a different region.

*Have each group report orally to the class.

*Make a poster or chart showing the Indian way of life.

Plains Indians	
clothing	food
shelter	tools and weapons

Then and Now

Have students compare the way Native Americans lived long ago and the way they live today. Make a booklet!

Long ago, Indians lived in . . .
Today they live . . .

Long ago, Indians got food . . .
Today they get food . . .

Long ago, Indians wore . . .
Today they wear . . .

Long ago, Indians played . . .
Today they play . . .

(You may want to use these activities when learning about Thanksgiving. See pages 27 and 28.)

Display books and pictures about Native Americans for students to peruse!

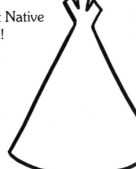

Shape Books

Write about Native Americans in a shape book.

©Frank Schaffer Publications, Inc.   FS-8305   Instant Idea Book

Native American Day

Make an Animal Hide

Have each student tear a piece of brown paper bag in a shape like an animal skin. Crumple it and smooth it out over and over. Repeat this until it feels like leather. Decorate with Indian designs.

Picture Language

Use Indian picture language to write messages!

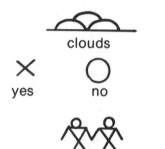

Indian Words in Our Language

Make a picture dictionary of Indian words used in our language today:

raccoon	moccasin
canoe	papoose
potato	chipmunk
tomato	opossum
moose	powwow

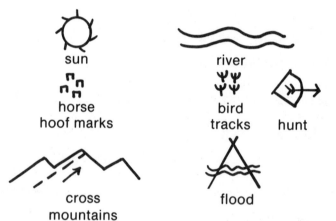

Clothing to Make

Some Native American tribes wore leather vests and headbands.

*Use a large, brown grocery sack to make a vest.

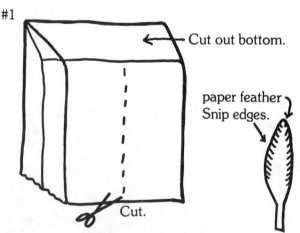

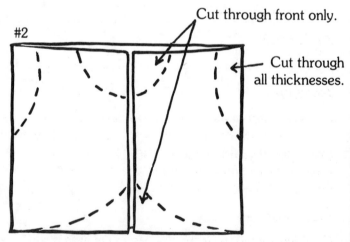

*Make a headband with a strip of paper.
 Add paper feathers.
 Staple or tape to fit head.

Fold bag with cut up center.
Cut on dotted lines.
Staple at shoulders.
Decorate and wear!

FS-8305   Instant Idea Book

Fire Prevention Week

The week that includes October 8, make your students aware of fire safety and prevention.

Communicate With Parents!

Inform parents that you are learning about fire safety. Explain to parents the importance of having a family evacuation plan in case of fire.

Ask parents to post emergency numbers by the telephone(s).

An Important Visitor!

Invite a representative from the fire department to talk to your class about fire safety. Perhaps you can take your class to visit the fire station.

Do you know how to report a fire?

Calling for Help!

Discuss with students the way to place an emergency phone call about a fire. Use role-playing to clarify the lesson. Have students make a roll movie about making an emergency phone call.

Fire Safety Rules

Discuss fire safety rules with students. Have each student make a poster (with a caption) about a fire safety rule.

At School

Leave the classroom in a quick, orderly manner during fire drills. Stay quiet and calm.

At Home

Don't have too many plugs in one outlet.
Don't play with matches. (Have a class discussion about what to do if a friend plays with matches.)
Store flammable liquids and rags in a safe place.
Use the stove and oven properly.
People should never smoke in bed.

Outdoors

Gasoline should never be used to make fires burn.
Make sure bonfires, campfires and barbecues are out.
Cigarettes should be crushed out.

©Frank Schaffer Publications, Inc.

FS-8305   Instant Idea Book

Columbus Day

On October 12, we honor Christopher Columbus (1451-1506) who was born in Italy. He sailed from Spain to a new land—"America." He landed on an island in the Bahamas which he named San Salvador.

Columbus' Ships

Columbus and his crew sailed on ships made of wood. They cooked food over a wood fire on the deck. The stars helped them know in which direction to sail. The Santa María, Niña and Pinta were powered by large sails.

- Compare ships of today with the ships used by Columbus.

- Make a three-dimensional picture of the kind of ship Columbus sailed.

  1. Draw the hull of the ship on brown paper.
  2. Cut out the hull and paste it on blue paper.
  3. Use strips of brown paper or crayons to make three masts on the ship.
  4. Cut sails from white paper and paste them on the ship. (Paste sails so they puff out.)
  5. Add details with crayons.

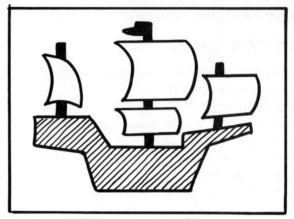

The Voyage of Columbus

Post a world map. Use a marking pen to indicate the route Columbus took on his first voyage to America.

Learn About Other Explorers!

Find out about other famous explorers who sailed the seas. Mark their routes on a world map.

The Life of Columbus

Assign each student to a partner. Give each pair of students a piece of 12″ x 18″ art paper. Assign each pair of students one event in the life of Columbus to illustrate. Post the pictures in sequence to tell the story of the life of Columbus.

Events to use:
1. Christopher Columbus was born in Italy in 1451.
2. He worked in his father's cloth-weaving shop.
3. He dreamed of becoming a sailor instead of a weaver.
4. He got a job on a ship.
5. He was living in Portugal in 1479. He got married.
6. He and his wife had a baby boy named Diego.
7. Columbus asked the king of Portugal for money to sail to India.
8. The king said, "No."
9. Columbus asked the queen and king of Spain for money to sail to India. The queen agreed to help Columbus in 1491.
10. They sailed on August 3, 1492.
11. Columbus saw birds and knew they were near land.
12. On October 12, he spotted land.
13. Columbus thought he reached India, so he called the people on the island "Indians." He named the island San Salvador.
14. Columbus returned to Spain in 1493.
15. Christopher Columbus died in 1506 after making four more trips to the new world.

©Frank Schaffer Publications, Inc.   FS-8305   Instant Idea Book

United Nations Day

This day commemorates the founding of the United Nations. It is celebrated on October 24. United Nations Headquarters in New York is a place where representatives from member nations meet to discuss problems.

The Melting Pot

Most Americans have ancestors who came from other parts of the world. Have students find out one of the countries that is in their ancestry. Post a world map on a bulletin board. Have each student make his face on a square of paper. Mount the "face squares" around the world map. Pin a strand of black yarn from each child's picture to a country in his ancestry.

★ ★
Information Please!

Write for information to:

UN Dept. of Public Information
United Nations
United Nations, New York 10017
★ ★

Hand-in-Hand

To foster a spirit of cooperation and brotherhood, make a bulletin board showing students' handprints in a circle.

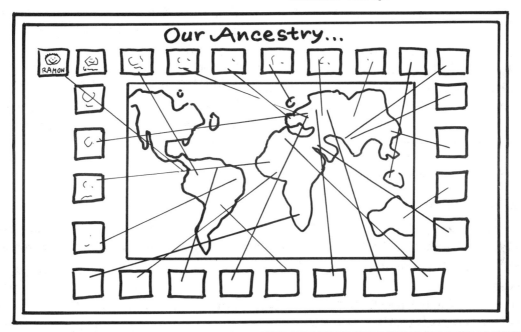

Our Ancestry...

Flags Around the World

Have each student make a flag from a different country. Post the flags in your classroom.

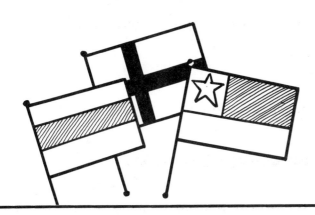

World Travel

Ask a travel agent to supply you with out-dated travel brochures to as many foreign countries as possible. Students can read the brochures and plan a trip to visit a country. Students may work individually or with a partner.

Halloween Fun

Spooky Shape Books

Let students choose a shape book for writing Halloween stories and poems.

Halloween Words

Use Halloween words for dictionary skills, sentence writing and stories:

Halloween	costume
October	mask
pumpkin	spider
jack-o'-lantern	monster
ghost	night
witch	moon
goblin	

Halloween Handwriting

Cut lined paper into Halloween shapes for handwriting practice.

Pumpkin Books

Write a sentence about Halloween on the chalkboard for students to copy. Then allow students to illustrate the sentence. Do a different sentence each day during the week before Halloween. Staple into booklets with orange covers.

Let's Write Poetry

Jot poetry starters on the board. Students may select one they like and write a Halloween poem.

The sky is dark,
The moon is bright . . .

Watch out for witches,
Stay away from ghosts . . .

I heard a sound,
I saw something move . . .

Run and hide,
It's Halloween night . . .

See the jack-o'-lantern,
Shining, oh, so bright . . .

I see yellow eyes,
What can it be . . .

Look at the sky,
What do you see . . .

The doorbell rang,
No one was there . . .

It's Halloween night,
Time for trick or treat . . .

©Frank Schaffer Publications, Inc.

FS-8305   Instant Idea Book

Halloween fun

How Pumpkins Grow

Have students fold a 12" x 18" paper three times. Number the sections from one to eight. List on the chalkboard what is to be drawn in each section.

1. Pumpkin seed is being planted.
2. Seed is getting water and sun.
3. Vine pops out of ground.
4. Vine grows longer.
5. Small green pumpkins appear.
6. Pumpkins grow large and turn orange.
7. Pumpkin gets picked.
8. Pumpkin becomes a jack-o'-lantern.

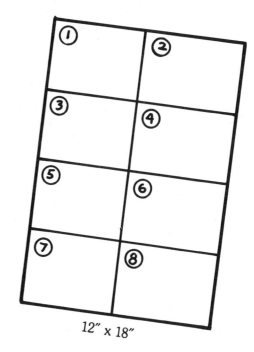

12" x 18"

Halloween Night Diorama

Have students paint the inside and outside of a shoe box black. When dry, add the moon and stars. Add a twig standing in clay to look like a tree. Add pumpkins, witches and ghosts (from paper scraps) to look like a scene on Halloween night.

The Class Pumpkin

Bring a pumpkin to school. Before carving the pumpkin, have students estimate the weight, circumference and number of seeds in the pumpkin.

Weigh the pumpkin to find the actual weight and announce which student made the closest estimate.

Use string to measure around the pumpkin at its widest point.

Carve the pumpkin and save the seeds to count, roast and eat.

Roasted Pumpkin Seeds

Rinse seeds. Simmer for 2 hours in 1 quart of water with 1 Tbsp. salt. Drain seeds and dry on paper towels. Spread seeds on cookie sheet with small amount oil. Bake at 250 degrees for 2 hours, stirring occasionally. Sprinkle lightly with salt and eat.

National Stamp Collector's Month!

In November, help your students become aware of the interesting hobby of stamp collecting.

Stamp Albums

Have each student make a construction paper booklet to use as a stamp album. Ask students to bring cancelled postage stamps to school from mail received at home. Show students how to remove stamps from paper by soaking in water. Students paste stamps in their albums. Duplicates are traded or placed in a box of extra stamps.

Design a Stamp!

Have students design a postage stamp for their school, city or state. *(See directions for super-size postage stamps on page 8.)*

Invite an Expert

Find out if a parent of one of your students is a stamp collector. Invite that person to share his/her collection with the class. Encourage students to share their stamp collections, too!

Stamps From Around the World

Buy an inexpensive packet of foreign stamps and a stamp album in a hobby or variety store. Encourage students who have stamp collections at home to bring duplicate stamps for the class album of foreign stamps.

Children's Book Week

The second full week of November is National Children's Book Week. Children's Book Week activities can also be used for National Library Week in April.

Instant Books

To get more books for your classroom library:

- Ask parents to donate books their children no longer read.
- Buy inexpensive used books at public library book sales.
- Tear apart old basal readers. Staple stories, adding tagboard covers. Students can decorate the "storybook" covers. (This is an excellent way of getting more books with controlled vocabulary levels.)

Public Libraries Are for Everyone!

Call the public library to find out about any special children's programs they offer. Inform students and parents! Let students know how easy it is to get a library card. Perhaps the librarian will visit your class to speak about library services.

Book Quilt

(Directions on page 6.)
Make a paper quilt from covers of favorite books or favorite story characters!

Fun and Fancy Bookmarks

Use yarn and construction paper to make bookmarks.

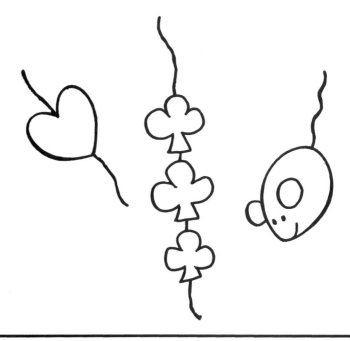

Children's Book Week

I-Read-a-Book Box

Establish an "I-Read-a-Book Box" in your classroom. Whenever students read a book (at home or school) and do a book-reporting activity, they earn recognition for reading. A perfect ongoing activity for extra credit work. Just what you need for students who are always the first to say, "I'm done!"

To avoid "lost" work-in-progress, provide a folder for each student.

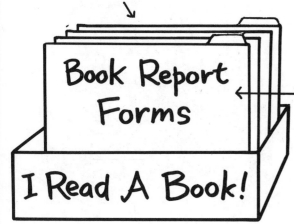

Keep book report forms handy!

I-Read-a-Book Activities!
(Choose one activity.)

1. Write a book report.
2. Make a diorama.
3. Make 2 bookmarks.
4. Write a letter to a friend about the book.
5. Make 3 pictures about the story. Show the beginning, middle and end.
6. Make a poster.
7. Make a book jacket, and write a summary on the back.
8. Make a sand table scene.
9. Write a different ending for the story.
10. Give an oral report about your book.

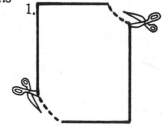 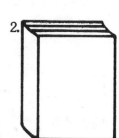

Two ideas for recognition for reading . . .

Book Train

Make a book train to show how many books your students read! Cut a locomotive from black paper and box cars from different colors of paper. Add a car to the book train each time a student reads a book. Put the book train on the wall above the chalkboard. It's fun to see how long the train becomes.

This also works well using paper figures!

Book Report Covers

Fold 12" x 18" construction paper in half. Cut off two corners to shape it like a book. Add lines, as shown, to make the folder look like a book. Cover can be decorated and book report stapled inside.

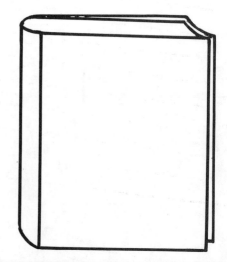

Thanksgiving

A time to think about the many things for which we are thankful.

Creative Writing Topics

I am thankful for . . .
Thanksgiving is a time for . . .
How my family celebrates Thanksgiving . . .

Thinking About Others

We are thankful for family and friends. Help your students share the gift of friendship with people who reside in a retirement home in your area. Have students write letters to senior citizen pen pals.

I Am Thankful

Hold a class discussion about the many things for which we are thankful. Follow the discussion with a writing activity.

Name _____
I am thankful for:
I _____
T _____
H _____
A _____
N _____
K _____
S _____
G _____
I _____
V _____
I _____
N _____
G _____

Words, Words, Words

Use these words for creative writing, or to make a word hunt, crossword puzzle or picture dictionary:

Thanksgiving	turkey
dinner	pumpkin pie
feast	cranberries
celebration	Pilgrims
harvest	Indians
family	thankful
food	

David is thankful for:
friends
family
good health
good food
church
school
my pets

Add colorful paper feathers to a construction paper turkey.

A Season for Sharing

Find out if your school (or class) can donate food to prepare food baskets for needy families.

CORN FLAKES

Thanksgiving

Then and Now

Study the way Pilgrims lived. Have students compare their lives to the lives of children long ago. Make a booklet!

Pilgrims got food
I get food . . .

Pilgrims played
I play . . .

Pilgrims got the news
I get the news from . . .

Pilgrims got clothes
I get clothes from . . .

Jobs Then and Now

Find out about jobs held by Pilgrims. Compare jobs of today to jobs long ago. Discuss how and why these careers have changed:

blacksmith
cobbler
cooper
weaver
town crier
tanner
tailor
wheelright
miller
silversmith
pewterer
barber
cabinet maker
clock maker

(You may want to use some ideas from Native American Day, pages 17 and 18.)

First Thanksgiving Mural

Put blue paper on a bulletin board (sky) and brown paper at the bottom to look like the ground. Discuss what the first Thanksgiving was like when the Pilgrims and Indians shared a feast. Have students draw and color an object to be cut out and stapled on the Thanksgiving mural.

Learning Activities for December, January, February and March

Winter activities

Jack Frost is here!

The Long, Cold Winter

Cut a long strip of white butcher paper (approximately fifteen feet long). Draw mountains, hills, trees and lakes. Then spread the paper out across the floor (or in the hallway) and have students get down on hands and knees along the paper. Students draw themselves having fun outdoors in the wintertime (sledding, skiing, ice skating, building snowmen). Post the winter mural for everyone to enjoy!

The Snow Is Falling!

Use 12" x 18" construction paper in shades of blue or use foil gift wrap. Fold paper in half 3 times. Then fan-fold on the creases. Cut triangle shapes out along folded edges, cutting through all thicknesses. Cut each end into a point. Fold and staple. Pull ends around to make snowflake and staple together. Spray lightly with spray snow!

Hang snowflakes from the ceiling, put on bulletin boards, or tape to windows to give your classroom a wintery look.

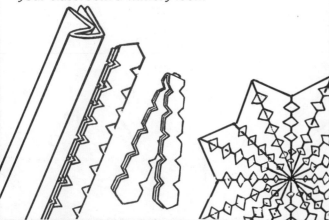

Stormy Days

A terrific project for a stormy, winter day. Paint white art paper (6" x 8"), using blues and tinges of purple to make a stormy, winter sky. Students should brush left to right and paint the entire paper. When dry, add wind-blown trees cut from black paper scraps. Mount "Stormy Day" pictures on a black background.

FS-8305   Instant Idea Book

Winter activities

Winter by the Yard

Give each student a strip of white paper measuring 2″ or 3″ x 36″. Students measure and follow directions for decorating their yard of white paper. (Begin measurement at "0".)

- 4 inches: Make a snowflake design.
- 3 inches: Write your name.
- 2 inches: Draw a left mitten.
  Color it blue and red.
- 7 inches: Draw Mr., Mrs. and "baby" Snowman.
- 2 inches: Draw a right mitten.
  Color it blue and red.
- 6 inches: Draw yourself in the snow.
- 3 inches: Draw a warm winter hat.
- 4 inches: Draw a pair of snow boots.
- 5 inches: Draw a scarf to keep you warm.
  Color it your favorite color.

Winter Poetry Starters

The wind is blowing,
It's cold out there . . .

When I woke up today,
The snow was coming down . . .

Winter is here,
I love the snow . . .

Mr. Snowman in the yard,
Standing all alone . . .

My nose is red,
My ears are cold . . .

Put on your hat,
Don't forget your boots . . .

Lace your ice skates,
Let's have some fun . . .

Hanukkah and Christmas

December is a holiday time when Hanukkah and Christmas are celebrated. Your students will enjoy these activities during the school days of December.

Holiday Countdown

Make a paper chain with twenty-five links of colored paper. At the end of each school day, one link is removed. Students can count the days (by counting the links) until Hanukkah, winter vacation from school and Christmas. If Hanukkah is December 4, make the fourth link on the paper chain in a different color. Do this also for the start of vacation time and Christmas.

Gifts From the Heart

Discuss doing something nice for a family member or friend instead of buying a gift. Have students think of a person they would like to do something special for. Students can draw pictures about this and write a sentence or paragraph about their "gift from the heart."

Hanukkah and Christmas

Holiday Creative Writing

Students will enjoy writing in a gift box shape book. Or draw a gift box on a master and duplicate a copy for each child. Students can write about:

- The Best Gift I Ever Received
- A Gift for Someone Special
- Something Special for You
- A Gift That Does Not Cost Money
- A Big Surprise

Holiday Celebrations at My House

Students can write about the way their families celebrate the holidays in a house shape book.

The Season for Sharing

Students can make greeting cards or holiday decorations to be delivered to a hospital, senior citizen center, nursing home, or hospital in your area.

©Frank Schaffer Publications, Inc.   FS-8305   Instant Idea Book

Hanukkah and Christmas

Holiday Words Picture Dictionary

Have each student make a picture dictionary of holiday words. Each word can be on a separate page with a colorful illustration. When all pages are done, they are arranged in alphabetical order and stapled into a booklet. Add and decorate construction paper covers. Older students can make holiday picture dictionaries for a primary class.

Words to use:

candle
reindeer
candy cane
stocking
dreidel
gifts
menorah
tree
wreath
Santa Claus
holly
bells
poinsettia
mistletoe
ornaments

Clay Dough Holiday Fun

Make holiday ornaments and decorations from clay dough. *(Directions for dough appear on page 6.)* The list of words for the holiday picture dictionary is also a list of objects to make from clay dough.

Braid
or
twist
clay
for wreath.

FS-8305 Instant Idea Book

Hanukkah and Christmas

Symbols of the Holiday Season

Primary students can make a book of holiday symbols with pictures to color and label. Do a different picture each day. Staple into a booklet for students to take home.

Older students can write sentences or a paragraph about each holiday symbol and draw an illustration.

(See the list of holiday words on page 34.)

Light-up Art

Duplicate a simple picture on construction paper. Students poke a series of pin holes to outline the picture. (Pin holes should be poked through picture on a piece of cardboard or pad of newspapers.) When pictures are hung in a window, light shines through the pin holes making a beautiful window decoration.

Dental Health Month

In February, help children learn how to keep their healthy, happy smiles!

Meet the Dentist!

Invite a dentist to speak to your class about dental care. Perhaps one of your students has a parent who is a dentist. Remind your students to visit the dentist twice a year.

Growing Up Strong and Healthy

Eating healthful foods makes strong, healthy teeth. Discuss good foods students should eat and sugary foods to avoid.

Have students keep track of between-meal snacks for one week.

Name _____
Snacks for the Week
Mon. _____
Tues. _____
Wed. _____
Thurs. _____
Fri. _____
Total: Healthful Snacks _____
      Not-so healthful snacks _____

Information Please!

Send for information:
American Dental Association
211 E. Chicago Ave.
Chicago, IL 60611

Healthy, Happy Smiles Bulletin Board

Divide a bulletin board in half. Students can post pictures of things that are helpful and harmful to dental health. (This activity can be done individually by students on a 12″ x 18″ piece of construction paper.)

How Often Do You Brush?

Have students keep track of brushing their teeth for one week.

Name _____
I brushed my teeth:
Mon. _____
Tues. _____
Wed. _____
Thurs. _____
Fri. _____

Taking Good Care of My Teeth

Have students make a mobile showing items that help keep their teeth healthy.

(See ideas for mobiles on page 8.)

Black History Month

Celebrate Black History Month in February with these learning activities.

Important Black Americans

Study the contributions of black people in many different fields. (The three names suggested in each category are not intended to be a complete list.)

(See additional ideas: pages 42 and 43, Famous Americans and page 47, Women's History.)

- Scientists & Inventors:

  Washington Carver
  Granville Woods
  Henry Blair

- Arts & Entertainment:

  Langston Hughes
  Duke Ellington
  Dr. Bill Cosby

- Government:

  Dr. Ralph J. Bunche
  Shirley Chisholm
  Julian Bond

- Sports:

  Jesse Owens
  O. J. Simpson
  Kareem Abdul-Jabbar

- Civil Rights:

  Dr. Martin Luther King, Jr.
  Harriet Tubman
  Frederick Douglass

Time Line

Make a time line showing important events in black history.

Learning About Black History

Make a picture book about a person in black history. Give the book to a student in a primary grade.

Black History Poster

Fold a 12″ x 18″ paper two times to get four sections. Trace a circle in the center of the paper. Make a poster about a person in black history. Draw the person and the dates of his or her birth/death in the circle. In each of the four sections, draw something important in that person's life.

Chinese New Year

Chinese New Year is a happy holiday. The date occurs between mid-January and mid-February.

"Gung Hay Fat Choy" Scroll

"Gung Hay Fat Choy" means Happy New Year in Chinese. Have each student make a banner on red paper that says "Happy New Year" in Chinese characters. Glue strips of black paper on the ends to make it look like a scroll.

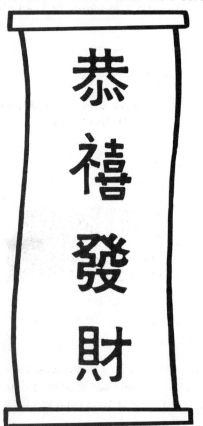

The Chinese Dragon

The Chinese dragon in the New Year parade is a symbol of strength and goodness. It is supposed to bring everyone good luck, peace and prosperity. Have your students make a dragon puppet. *(Quickie paper puppet directions are on page 8.)*

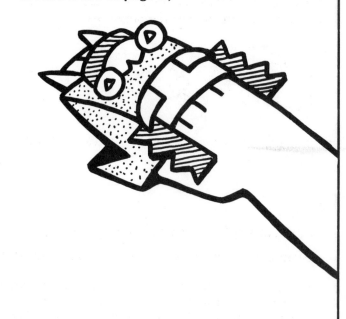

Chinese Writing

Children enjoy learning to write the numbers from one to ten in Chinese characters. This should be done with a brush and ink or paint.

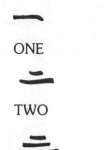

一	四	七	十
ONE	FOUR	SEVEN	TEN
二	五	八	
TWO	FIVE	EIGHT	
三	六	九	
THREE	SIX	NINE	

Groundhog Day

Groundhog Day is February 2!

There is an old superstition that if the groundhog can see his shadow on February 2 there will be six more weeks of winter. Scientists know that the groundhog's shadow does not really tell what the weather will be like. However, it is still fun to see if the groundhog weather forecast comes true!

Groundhog Weather Forecasts

For six weeks following Groundhog Day, mark the weather each day on the classroom calendar. At the end of six weeks, discuss with your students how true the groundhog's forecast was.

Use weather symbols to mark the calendar and record the high and low temperatures.

sunny　snowy　windy　rainy　cloudy

Learn About Groundhogs

Groundhogs are really animals called woodchucks. Have your students find out about woodchucks.

Animals That Hibernate

Learn about other animals that hibernate, such as frogs, chipmunks, bats and bears.

Collecting Weather Data

Weather conditions are good subjects for students to observe and record.

• Start a record book of weather. Have a student write what the weather is like or clip and paste the weather report from the newspaper. Save this book, so your next year's students can compare today's weather with the next year's weather.

• Use a thermometer to measure the temperature at the same time of day, each day. Record the results on a graph.

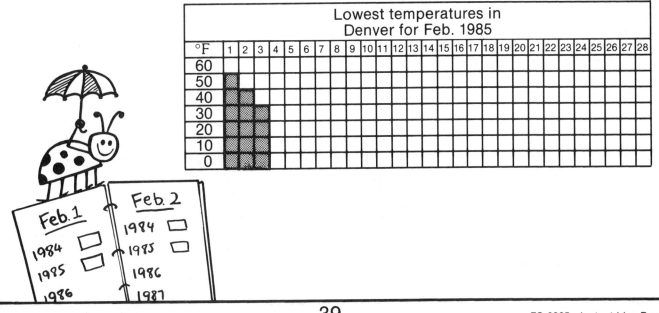

Lowest temperatures in Denver for Feb. 1985

FS-8305　Instant Idea Book

Valentine's Day

This is a special day for thinking about people we love.

A Very Special Valentine's Gift

Cut a heart from pink paper for each student. Or, use a duplicating master and run off on pink paper. Use these hearts as rewards or as a valentine card from teacher to students.

To _____

From _____

10 MINUTES OF FREE TIME

Special People at Our School

Make valentine cards for special people in your school:

bus driver
cafeteria helpers
custodian
librarian
secretary
principal
nurse

For me?

Heart Handwriting

Use heart-shaped paper for handwriting practice on Valentine's Day.

Recycle Valentine Cards

Cut the colored picture from the front of a card into two or three puzzle pieces. Pop the pieces into an envelope. Give each student a valentine puzzle to put together and paste on a paper.

FS-8305 Instant Idea Book

Valentine's Day

Nice People in Our Class

On February 1, decorate an envelope or box with hearts. Whenever you or your students observe someone in the class doing something thoughtful, write a note about that person and what they did, and put it in the box. On Valentine's Day, read aloud the "nice notes" that are in the box.

The Name Exchange

Exchange class lists with another teacher at your school. Let each child draw a name of a student in the other class. Then, that child makes a valentine card for the person whose name he drew.

Silent Observer

Put the names of everyone in the class (teacher, too) in an envelope. Each person draws a name and keeps the name a secret. Tell students to observe the person whose name they drew during the morning. After lunch, have students write two positive observations about that person. Post on a bulletin board or allow students to read aloud, having students guess the name.

Valentine Word List

valentine
card
paper
lace
deliver
love
cupid
red
white
pink
heart
cupid

A Very Special Friend

K-1: Draw a picture of yourself and your best friend. Dictate a sentence to the teacher to write under your picture.

2-6: Have students write about one friend. Tell how they met and became friends. Tell what they like to do together.

41

President's Day

President's Day is the third Monday of February. February is a perfect month to study famous Americans including Abraham Lincoln and George Washington.

If I Were President

Have students write about what they would do if they were president of our country. You might want to send the students' writings to the White House in Washington, D.C.

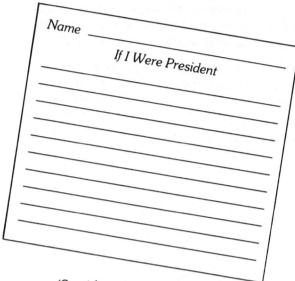

Name _____

If I Were President

(See ideas for patriotic holidays on page 63.)

```
* * * * * * * * * * * * * * *
*                            *
*     Information Please!     *
*     Have students write to: *
*       Office of President    *
*       c/o The White House    *
*       Washington, D. C.      *
*                  20001       *
*                            *
* * * * * * * * * * * * * * *
```

Design a Commemorative Stamp!

Have students design a postage stamp about a famous American. *(Directions for making stamps appear on page 8.)*

Sally Ride

Famous Americans' Quilt

Make a paper quilt of famous Americans with birth/death dates under each picture. *(Directions for paper quilts appear on page 6.)*

Famous Americans

FS-8305   Instant Idea Book

President's Day

Famous American Reports

Assign each student a different famous American about whom to write a report. Post a time line, so each student can indicate the birth date of the person about whom he wrote.*

To aid report writing, you might want to give students a note-taking form for gathering information. Then they use that form for writing the report. This makes it a bit less likely that the reports will be copied from reference books.

Notes About

_____

Born: _____ Died: _____

Place of Birth: _____

About family

_____

_____

About childhood

_____

_____

Why is he/she famous?

_____

_____

_____

How did he/she get to be famous?

_____

_____

_____

*

Time Lines

Have each student make a time line showing important events in the life of a famous person.

Guess Who?

Have students report orally on the famous people they studied. Each student should give information but not reveal the name of the person. After hearing important information about the person, the class tries to guess the identity.

FS-8305   Instant Idea Book

National Nutrition Month

In March, help your students grow up strong and healthy by eating well and staying fit.

Good Nutrition Bulletin Board

Have students cut pictures from old magazines and put them on the bulletin board under the correct food group.

Food Advertising

Show samples of newspaper and magazine ads for foods. Discuss television advertising for foods and restaurants. Talk about how advertising makes us want to buy certain foods.

A Food Log

Have students keep track of everything they eat in a twenty-four hour period. Have students discuss what foods they could have eliminated or substituted for better nutrition.

Fitness Counts!

Have each student keep track of his/her exercise activities for one week. Discuss ways to increase exercise.

Super Chef

Have students plan foods to be eaten for a nutritious breakfast, lunch and dinner.

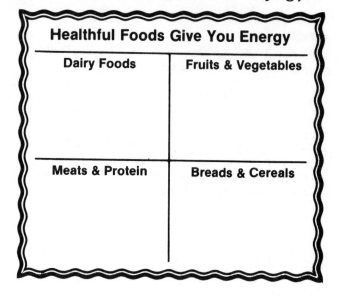

Healthful Foods Give You Energy	
Dairy Foods	Fruits & Vegetables
Meats & Protein	Breads & Cereals

FS-8305 Instant Idea Book

National Nutrition Month

Strong and Healthy Posters

Have each student design a poster about good nutrition or fitness. Decorate the classroom or school cafeteria with the posters.

Good Foods Mobile

Have students make a four-food-groups mobile or a mobile of healthful snack foods.

Grow Some Sprouts

You will need:
- 2 quart jars
- 2 rubber bands
- 2 squares of clean cheesecloth or nylon (cut from stockings)
- alfalfa seeds for sprouting
- water

- **Day 1:** Put 2 tablespoons of alfalfa seeds in each jar. Cover with water and soak overnight.
- **Day 2:** Cover tops of jars with cheesecloth secured with rubber bands. Drain.
- **Put** jars on their sides away from sunlight. Rinse three times a day. Drain well after each rinse.
- **Day 3 and 4:** Continue to rinse and drain until jars are almost filled with growing sprouts.
- **Day 4 or 5:** Place jar on windowsill to expose to sunlight. Sprouts will turn green. Then they are ready to eat.
- **Have** students put sprouts on sandwiches or on stuffed celery.
- **Encourage** students to grow sprouts for their families to use on sandwiches and salads.

Good Nutrition Placemats

Students can make a set of placemats using 12" x 18" construction paper. Placemats can be decorated with a good nutrition theme and used at home.

FS-8305   Instant Idea Book

Bird Day and Arbor Day

March 7 is the birthday of Luther Burbank, famous American naturalist. Bird Day and Arbor Day are celebrated on different dates. In many places, they are celebrated on the anniversary of Luther Burbank's birth.

A Famous Naturalist

Luther Burbank experimented with plants. He developed many new trees, plants and fruits. Have your students make an informational poster about Luther Burbank.

Fold 12" x 18" or 9" x 12" paper two times.

Feathered Friends

Gather a collection of bird books that show full color pictures of birds. Identify as many birds as possible that live in your area. Make a bulletin board showing your feathered friends.

Our Neighborhood Trees

Identify as many trees as possible that grow in your area. Make a class book showing neighborhood trees.

Learning Bookmarks

Give each student a strip of tagboard (approximately 3" x 12"). Each student draws a bird in full color, labels it and writes a sentence on the bookmark. Bookmarks are placed in a box where everyone can use them. You can also do this for trees and plants.

Bird Identification Contest

Put colored pictures of birds on a bulletin board. Number the pictures. Students identify as many birds as possible on their answer sheets. Award a prize to the student who correctly identifies the most birds.

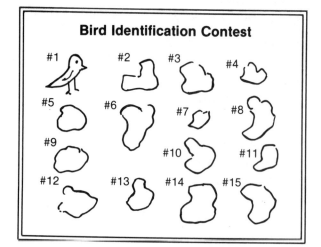

Trees Through the Seasons

Students fold their papers two times. Each section is labelled with a different season. Students draw a tree as it appears in each season.

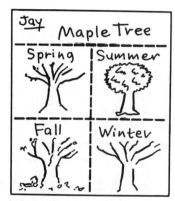

Trees Are Important!

Discuss with your class the many ways trees help other living things. Make a list on the chalkboard.

Women's History Week

Celebrate Women's History Week the week of March 8.

Learning About Important Women in History

Study the many different contributions made by women. (The three names suggested in each category are not intended to be a complete list.)

- Scientists & Inventors:
  Florence Sabin
  Amelia Earhart
  Rachel Louise Carson

- Arts & Entertainment:
  Mary Cassatt
  Helen Hayes
  Marian Anderson

- Government:
  Eleanor Roosevelt
  Margaret Chase Smith
  Shirley Chisholm

- Sports:
  Mildred "Babe" Didrikson Zaharias
  Billie Jean King
  Mary Lou Retton

- Civil Rights:
  Harriet Tubman
  Florence Sanger
  Susan B. Anthony

(For additional activities, see: page 37, Black History Month and page 42 and 43 Famous Americans.)

Important Questions

Ask students to interview their mothers, aunts, or grandmothers to learn about:

- her family when she was young
- her elementary school
- what she did after school
- the kinds of jobs she held
- what hobbies she enjoyed
- what chores she did at home
- how things are different for girls now than when she was young.

An Important Woman in Your Life

Ask students to select women who have had an influence upon them. Have each student think of something about that person (mother, grandmother, aunt. . .) that could make her famous. Each student writes a paragraph telling who the person is and why she would be famous. Students can draw a picture to illustrate their writing.

Kindergarten and first grade students can dictate a sentence to the teacher to go with their picture.

©Frank Schaffer Publications, Inc. FS-8305 Instant Idea Book

National Wildlife Week

In March, help your students learn about animals and vegetation in your area.

Words to Learn

Use these words for dictionary work, alphabetizing and sentence writing activities:

hibernate
migrate
environment
habitat
mammal
reptile
amphibian

★ ★

Information Please!

For information, write:

National Wildlife Federation
1412 16th Street, NW
Washington, DC 20036

★ ★

Wildlife in Your Area

Find out what kinds of animals live in your area or state in the wild. Are any of these living things in danger of extinction?

Creative Writing

Students can write a story about a day in the life of a plant or animal at your school.

Animal Classification

Have your students draw and label an animal from each class of vertebrates:

fish
birds
mammals
reptiles
amphibians

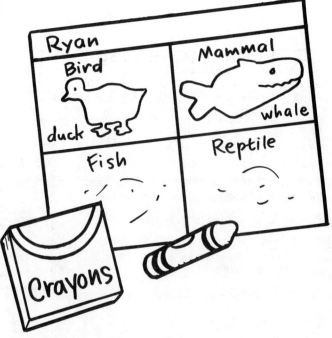

St. Patrick's Day

Irish people loved St. Patrick and honor him on March 17, the day of his death.

Special Shamrocks

Each student needs 12" x 18" white art paper. Students draw a large shamrock on the paper. Or, you can provide a shamrock template for students to trace. Using various shades of green paper, students cut out circles about the size of a quarter. Circles are pasted on the big shamrock, scattering the various shades of green. When the big shamrock is "covered" with green, outline it with a dark green crayon. Add a decorative border to this special shamrock.

Lucky Shamrocks

Cut out dozens of small shamrocks from green construction paper. Write a word relating to St. Patrick's Day on each shamrock. Put the shamrocks in a bag or envelope. Add a few lucky shamrocks that do not have a word written on them. Let each student reach in and take three shamrocks. Students write a sentence for each word they chose. If they pick a lucky shamrock without a word, they only write two sentences. When writing sentences, students paste the shamrock in the sentence instead of writing the word.

Wearing-of-the-Green Handwriting

Paste lined paper cut into a shamrock shape on a green paper background. Have students copy a sentence from the board in their best handwriting.

Ideas for Sentences:

- Be sure to wear green on March 17.
- Today is St. Patrick's Day.
- Irish people loved St. Patrick.
- Have you ever seen a leprechaun?

FS-8305   Instant Idea Book

Learning Activities for April, May and June

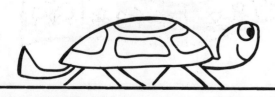  

Spring activities

Spring is here! The month of March comes in like a lion and goes out like a lamb, bringing the first warm days of spring.

More Daylight Every Day

Record daily temperatures, and sunrise and sunset times on your classroom calendar. Discuss the changing weather patterns.

The Signs of Spring

Start a list of signs of spring on the chalkboard. Ask students to tell you when they notice new signs of spring, so they may be added to the list. Take a nature walk around the school grounds to look for signs of spring.

Signs of Spring by the Yard

Measurement and following directions skills are included in this interesting activity. Give each student a strip of white paper 3″ x 36″. Write directions on the chalkboard for measuring and decorating the strip. (Begin measurement at "0".)

Measure:

- 3 inches: Write your name.
- 4 inches: Draw a rainbow.
- 6 inches: Draw an umbrella and raindrops design.
- 7 inches: Write "SPRING IS HERE" in your favorite spring color.
- 2 inches: Draw the sun.
- 5 inches: Make a bird's nest with two baby birds.
- 6 inches: Draw spring flowers.
- 3 inches: Draw a butterfly.

It's Planting Time

Plant some seeds to grow on a sunny windowsill. When weather permits, students can take the plants home and plant them outdoors. Use milk cartons and containers from eggs, yogurt, and cottage cheese as planters. Plant hardy seeds such as marigolds or zucchini.

Grow an Avocado Tree

Put an avocado seed in a jar of water with toothpicks. When roots grow, plant it in a flowerpot.

A Carrot Garden

Grow carrot tops in a shallow dish of water on a sunny windowsill. This also works with tops from beets, turnips, and pineapples. What fun to watch them grow.

Adopt-a-Tree

Choose a tree to observe carefully. Keep a log of the date that you looked at the tree and the changes you observed for four weeks.

FS-8305   Instant Idea Book

Spring activities

Seeds Are Strong

Show your class how strong seeds are when they are growing. Fill a small plastic container with bean or pea seeds. Cover the seeds with water and cover the jar with a lid. Use a rubber band to hold the lid on the jar. After about a day, the seeds will have swelled from the water, and the container's lid will pop. (A clear plastic or glass jar works best, so students can see the seeds increasing in size.)

The Forsythia Is Blooming

Put blue background paper on a bulletin board. Draw or use brown paper strips to add bare branches for the forsythia bush. Cut yellow construction paper in strips measuring 2″ x ½″. Allow a few students at a time to come up to the bulletin board to paste the yellow flowers on the forsythia. Flowers are pasted on by criss-crossing two yellow strips. They should be pasted in the middle only, so the ends can be turned up. You will have a beautiful forsythia in your classroom to announce the coming of spring.

Invite an Expert

Invite someone from a local nursery to tell your class about the best kinds of plants, fruits and vegetables to grow in your area. Perhaps the visitor will do a demonstration on how to plant seeds. Find out what nurseries do with unsold, outdated seeds at end of season. Perhaps businesses will donate them to your class. Even though they are last year's batch of seeds, you will get good results.

A Sponge Planter

Wet a large sponge and squeeze out the water. Sprinkle the sponge with seeds (grass, clover, or mustard). Moisten and the seeds will sprout.

FS-8305   Instant Idea Book

Bicycle Safety Month

April is a time to remind students of safety rules to use all year long.

Bicycle Safety Booklet

Have each student make a booklet about bicycle safety.

Important Bicycle Safety Rules

- Bicycle riders must obey all traffic rules.
- Bicycle riders should use the same hand signals for slowing down and turning that drivers use.
- Ride on the right-hand side of the street (same as cars).
- Walk bikes across busy streets.
- Be sure your bike is in good condition. Check brakes, tires and reflectors.
- Bicycle riders should wear protective clothing (helmets and reflective colors).

Safe Bicyclist Certificate

After studying bicycle safety, give each student a certificate!

Invite an expert!

Invite someone from a local bike repair shop to bring a bicycle and show students how to check tires and brakes. And, show students where reflectors should be on bicycles for optimum safety.

Cycle City

Construct a table top display using butcher paper and boxes for buildings. Draw roads, bike lanes and intersections on butcher paper. Add buildings and traffic signs (paper signs on a straw or popsicle stick standing in small lump of clay). Have students draw and cut out a bike rider. Have students "ride" their bikes along the streets of Cycle City obeying bike safety rules.

★ ★

Information Please!

Information on bicycle safety is available from:

National Safety Council
Youth Department
444 N. Michigan Ave.
Chicago, IL 60611

★ ★

FS-8305   Instant Idea Book

April Fools' Day

This is a special day for playing tricks that are fun for everyone.

An April Fools' Cartoon Strip

Fold 12" x 18" construction paper two times to make four sections. Number the sections from 1 to 4. Students can make a cartoon strip showing an April Fools' trick.

Joke Books

On April Fools' Day, we think of tricks, riddles and jokes. Make a booklet of riddles and/or jokes. Staple paper into a booklet or make an accordian book. *(Directions on page 7.)*

April Fools' Fun

Divide students into groups of three or four. Have each group act out an April Fools' trick for the class.

It Happened to Me

At the end of the school day on April Fools' Day, allow students to tell the class about tricks that happened at school that day.

FS-8305 Instant Idea Book

Easter

It's time for Easter!

Easter Mobile

Have students make a mobile of Easter objects: eggs, bunny, chick, basket.

Eggshell Flowers

Save broken (not blown) eggshells. Place eggshells in an egg carton and fill shells with dirt. Plant a seed for a spring flower in each eggshell and place in a sunny place. Water daily. When it is warm enough outdoors, flowers can be planted outside. When planting, leave the plant in the eggshell.

Fingerprint Fun

Students can make cute animals using fingerprints (from tempera or a stamp pad) to use for artwork or greeting cards.

Clay Dough Critters

Make bunnies, chicks, lambs, ducks and eggs from clay dough. *(See recipe on page 6.)*

FS-8305   Instant Idea Book

Keep America Beautiful Week

The third full week of April, is a perfect time to study ecology. Students will learn how living things relate to each other and to the world around them.

Recycle Trash

Find out about recycling facilities in your community. Encourage students to talk to their families about recycling as many items as possible.

Litter Hurts Our Environment

Organize a school-wide, anti-litter campaign to keep school grounds free of litter. Have students make and post anti-litter signs at school.

Have each student use a grocery bag to make a litter bag for the family car. Students can decorate the bag with an ecology theme.

How You Can Help!

Discuss ways students can help our world by saving energy. Make a list on the chalkboard:

>   Take short showers.
>   Ride bikes instead of riding in cars.
>   Don't waste paper.
>   Don't litter.
>   Turn off lights or TV when not using.
>   Recycle trash.
>   Don't waste water.

Energy Reminders

Have students make small signs to use at home to help family members remember to save energy.

Ecology Begins Right Here

Discuss with your class ways you can save energy in your classroom. Make a list on the chalkboard.

Keep America Beautiful Week

Advice From the Experts

Telephone your power company to find out if they have free literature about saving energy. Get enough copies so each student can take home information about saving energy.

Important Words

Introduce vocabulary words to your class for spelling, dictionary or sentence writing activities:

> ecology
> environment
> pollution
> biodegradable
> natural resource

Ecology Bookmarks

Each student can design a bookmark with a "KEEP AMERICA BEAUTIFUL" theme. Give the bookmarks to the school librarian or to another class to use.

Save-a-Tree

Establish a box for scrap paper. When students need scratch paper, they can get it from the scratch paper box.

FS-8305   Instant Idea Book

Be Kind to Animals Week

Celebrate "Pets Are Wonderful Month" in April and "Be Kind to Animals Week" in May. The activities on this page will help you enjoy either of these special holidays about animals.

Graph of Our Pets

Make a graph on butcher paper. Have students color a box for each pet they have. Add the totals.

Our Pets																		TOTAL
dog			▨	▨	▨	▨	▨											
cat			▨	▨	▨													
fish			▨	▨														
turtle			▨															
rabbit			▨															
hampster			▨															
rat																		

My Favorite Animal

Each student should choose an animal about which to write. It can be his own pet.
Students can:

- Write about the animal.
- Draw or paint a picture of the animal.
- Do a time line showing a typical day in the life of the animal.
- Make a clay model of the animal.
- Write a poem about the animal.
- Look up factual information about the animal in the encyclopedia.

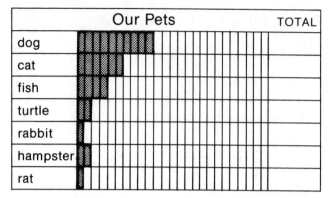

Be Kind to Animals

Discuss what animals need:
    good food
    exercise
    clean air and water
    love and kindness
    good care

Have students make a poster to encourage kindness to animals.

Invite an Expert!

Invite a veterinarian or someone from an animal shelter to talk with your class about animals.

FS-8305 Instant Idea Book

National Family Week

This special family week is the first full week of May. Mother's day is celebrated on the second Sunday in May. The third Sunday of June is Father's Day.

My Family

Students draw a house on 12" x 18" construction paper. Each student cuts a door and windows, and shapes the roof. Paste a piece of white paper behind the "house". Open the windows and door and draw family members.

Cinquain Poetry

Cinquain poetry is unrhymed and is perfect for writing about parents or family.

Line 1: one word (can be the title)
Line 2: two words (describe the title)
Line 3: three words (an action)
Line 4: four words (a feeling)
Line 5: one word (referring to title)

Very Special Coupons

Students can make a booklet of coupons for mother, father, or family. Elicit a list of ideas from students to jot on chalkboard. Then let students select 8 items to include in their coupon booklets. Add colorful construction paper covers to the booklets.

A Note of Appreciation

Each student writes a note of appreciation to mother, father, or family member. The note mentions something that he appreciates that has happened recently.

Examples:

Family
Busy, happy
Like to ski
Like to be together
Johnsons

Mother
Pretty, busy
Sews and cooks
Is a happy person
Nancy

Ideas to include:

wash the car
water plants
cut lawn
do the dishes
take out the trash
set the table
make your bed
dust
feed our pets
put away groceries
help prepare dinner

May Day

May Day signals the beginning of spring. It is a time when the world outside is beginning to bloom.

May Baskets

Fill a May basket with fresh or paper flowers. Decorate a plastic berry basket by weaving yarn in spring colors in and out of the openings. You can also use construction paper strips.

Make a paper basket from construction paper or wallpaper. Decorate a 12" x 12" square of construction paper with a flower design. Paste or staple two corners together. Add a handle and fill with flowers.

Friendly Flowers

Cut squares of paper in assorted colors (red, yellow, pink, purple, orange) and assorted sizes (6" x 6", 5" x 5", 4" x 4", 3" x 3"). Cut light pink or flesh-colored circles to use for flower centers.

Each student selects three squares in various colors and sizes. To make flowers, fold each square 2 times. Then fold, bringing two corners together to make a triangle. Cut edges to make round petal shape and unfold. (You may need to cut the petal shape for students as student scissors are not sharp enough to cut through several thicknesses of paper.) Students paste flowers on light blue 12" x 18" art paper. A pink circle is pasted in the center of each flower. Students draw a face on each flower center. Stems and leaves can be added with green crayon or paper scraps.

Cinco de Mayo

The fifth of May is a national holiday in Mexico. It is a celebration of winning a battle with French soldiers who were invading Mexico.

Do You Speak Spanish?

Teach your students Spanish words for colors and numbers.
Make a Spanish/English dictionary.

rojo	red	1	uno
amarillo	yellow	2	dos
verde	green	3	tres
azúl	blue	4	cuatro
negro	black	5	cinco
moreno	brown	6	seis
morado	purple	7	siete
blanco	white	8	ocho
anaranjado	orange	9	nueve
		10	diez

Fiesta Time

At many Mexican holiday celebrations, children break open a piñata to get candy and coins from inside the animal. An easy way to make a piñata is to use a large brown grocery sack. Cut strips of crepe paper (approximately 2″ wide) in bright colors. Have students cut the crepe paper, so it is fringed. Stuff the bag with crumpled newspaper. Have students paste crepe paper fringe around the bag until the bag is completely covered. Add candy and pennies and tie the piñata shut.

When checking students' work, write *Muy bueno* (very good) or *Buen trabajo* (good work) on papers.

Crepe Paper Artwork

Precut 1½″ squares of crepe paper in many bright colors. Each child draws a simple object (bird, flower, butterfly) on a 9″ x 12″ piece of construction paper. Students mold a square of crepe paper around the end of a pencil, remove and twist bottom. Crepe paper "twistees" are pasted all over the object.

FS-8305   Instant Idea Book

Japanese Children's Day

This day is celebrated May 5. It is a national holiday in Japan. This is a special day when parents give thanks for their children.

Carp Kites

You will need:

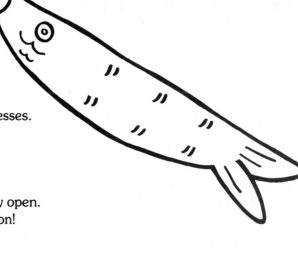

> butcher paper (18" x 24")
> strip of tagboard (1" x 12")
> glue
> newspaper
> paints, crayons or felt markers

- Fold butcher paper in half lengthwise.
- Draw and cut out fish cutting through both thicknesses. (Do not cut along the fold.)
- Color the carp on both sides with bright colors.
- Staple, leaving the mouth and tail open.
- When fish is stuffed, staple tail.
- Glue strip of tagboard inside mouth to make it stay open.
- Attach string and hang as Children's Day decoration!

Make a Japanese Miniature Garden (Bon Kei)

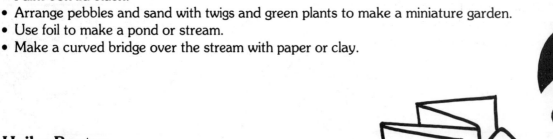

You will need:

> a shoe box lid
> black paint
> small rocks, pebbles and sand, or kitty litter
> small piece of aluminum foil
> twigs
> small parts of green shrubs to look like miniature trees/bushes
> modeling clay (to hold plants)

- Paint box lid black.
- Arrange pebbles and sand with twigs and green plants to make a miniature garden.
- Use foil to make a pond or stream.
- Make a curved bridge over the stream with paper or clay.

Haiku Poetry

Write a Haiku poem about Japanese gardens.
Haiku poetry does not have to rhyme.

> **Line 1:** 5 syllables
> **Line 2:** 7 syllables
> **Line 3:** 5 syllables

(Haiku poems can be written in an accordian book. See page 7.)

Flag Day

June 14 marks the anniversary of June 14, 1777 when the Congress resolved that the flag would have thirteen stripes, alternating red and white, and there would be thirteen stars on a blue field.

The Stars and Stripes

Red stands for courage, blue for justice, and white for purity on our flag. Have students use construction paper to make a flag.

Patriotic Patchwork

(Follow directions for paper quilts on page 6.)

Have each student make a quilt square that shows a patriotic symbol. Use red or blue for the quilt background.

Symbols:
drum and drumsticks
national seal
flag of 1777
flag of today
Liberty Bell
Statue of Liberty

State Posters

Have each student make a poster about a different state. Fold a 12″ x 18″ paper two times to get four sections. Each student writes the name of the state in one section, and illustrates that state's bird, flower and flag in the other sections. Have students label the state birds and flowers.

United States Postage Stamp

Students can design a patriotic stamp for the United States. *(See directions on page 8.)*

Flags of Our Country

Have each student make a flag of a different state. Students who work quickly can make an additional flag, so you have a set of all fifty flags. Display the flags on a banner or a bulletin board.